SEA LIFE

CLOWN FISH

by **Mari Schuh**

Consulting Editor:
Gail Saunders-Smith, PhD

Consultant:
Jody Rake, Member,
Southwest Marine Educators Association

CAPSTONE PRESS
a capstone imprint

Pebble Plus is published by Capstone Press,
1710 Roe Crest Drive, North Mankato, Minnesota 56003
www.capstonepub.com

Library of Congress Cataloging-in-Publication Data
Schuh, Mari C.
Clown Fish / by Mari Schuh.
p. cm.—(Pebble Plus. Sea Life)
Summary: "Describes the characteristics, food, habitat, and behavior of clown fish"—Provided by publisher.
Audience: Ages 5–8.
Audience: K to grade 3.
Includes bibliographical references and index.
ISBN 978-1-4914-6042-9 (library binding)
ISBN 978-1-4914-6062-7 (eBook PDF)
1. Anemonefishes—Juvenile literature. I. Title.
QL638.P77S45 2016
597'.72—dc23   2014049349

Editorial Credits
Elizabeth R. Johnson, editor; Aruna Rangarajan, designer;
Kelly Garvin, media researcher; Tori Abraham, production specialist

Photo Credits
Minden Pictures/Yoji Okata/Nature Production, 21; Shutterstock: Andra Izzotti, 7, artefacti, 8, Godruma, cover (background), Kim Briers, 15, Kletr, cover, Krzysztof Odziomek, 5, Levent Konuk, 11, Nadieh Schellekens, 13, Rich Carey, 9, SARAWUT KUNDEJ, 19, Sergey Novikov, 17

Design Elements: Shutterstock: SusIO, Vectomart

Note to Parents and Teachers

The Sea Life set supports national science standards related to life science. This book describes and illustrates clown fish. The images support early readers in understanding the text. The repetition of words and phrases helps early readers learn new words. This book also introduces early readers to subject-specific vocabulary words, which are defined in the Glossary section. Early readers may need assistance to read some words and to use the Table of Contents, Glossary, Read More, Internet Sites, and Index sections of the book.

Printed in China by Nordica
0415/CA21500542
032015   008837NORDF15

Table of Contents

Life in the Ocean

Clown fish dart through the warm ocean water. These bright orange fish live in small groups.

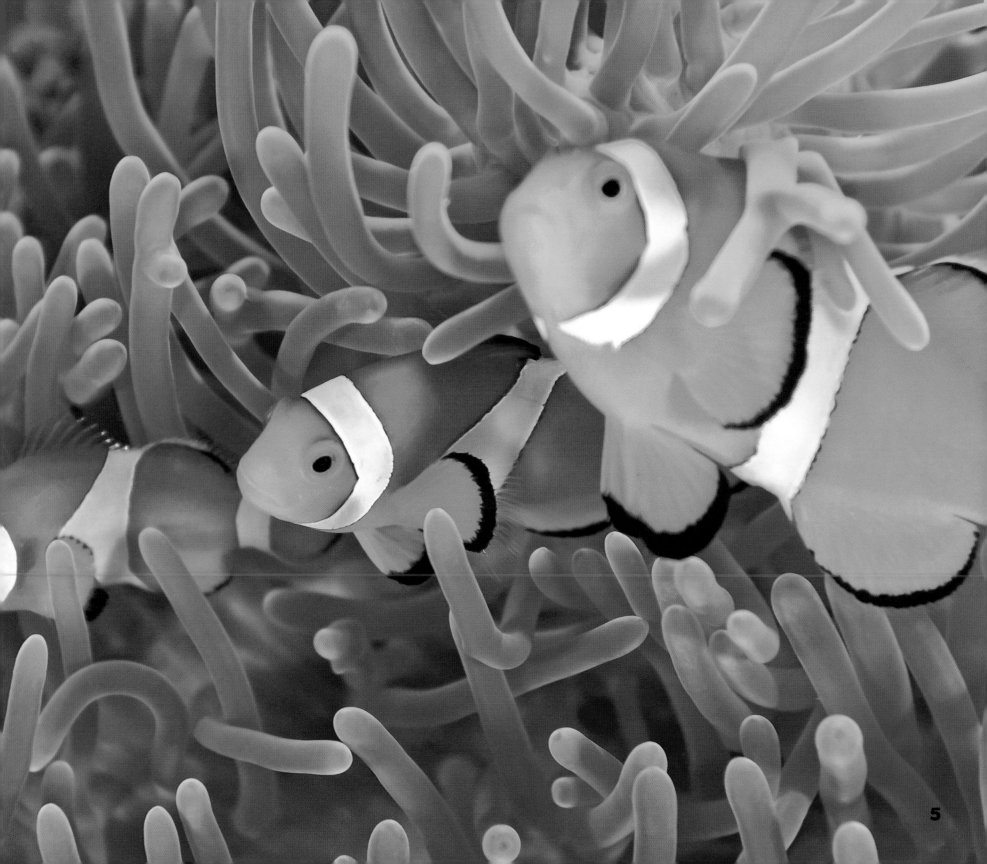

Clown fish are about 4 inches
(10 centimeters) long.
They get their name from
their bold colors.
The colors look like a
clown's face paint.

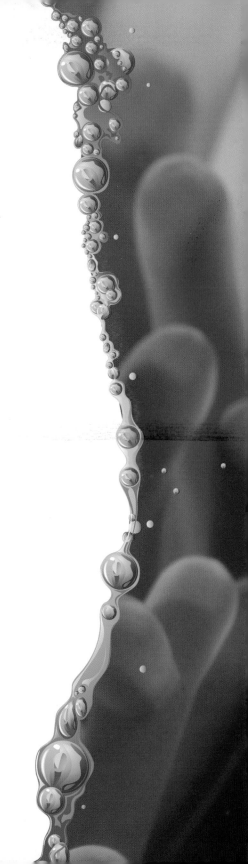

Clown fish swim in the Pacific and Indian oceans.
They live in coral reefs.

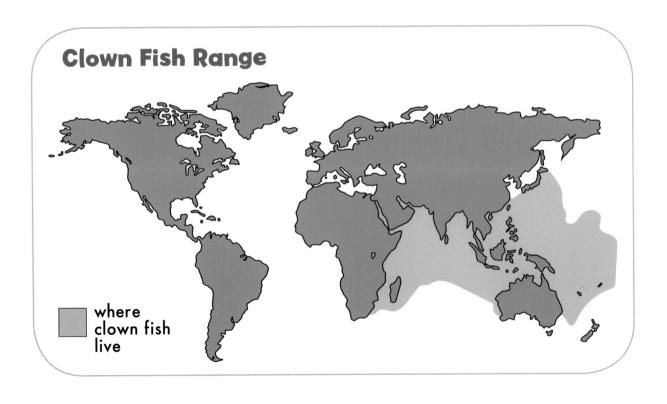

Clown Fish Range

where clown fish live

A Safe Place to Live

Clown fish make their home in sea anemones.
Sea anemones are animals with many tentacles.

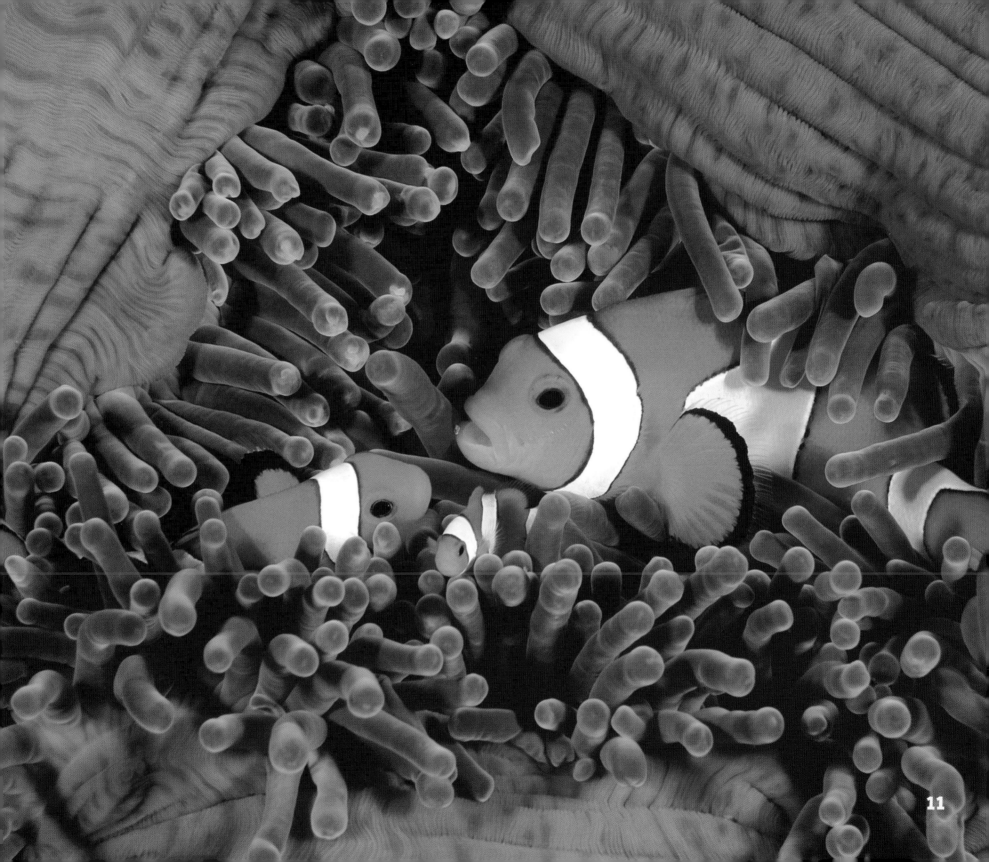

The tentacles have stingers
that hurt and kill fish.
But clown fish are safe.
Clown fish have a special slime
on their scales that protects them.

Working Together

Clown fish and sea anemones help each other. Sea anemones protect clown fish from predators. Clown fish scare away fish that might eat sea anemones.

Clown fish keep sea anemones clean. When the anemone eats a fish, the clown fish eats the leftover pieces. Clown fish eat dead anemone tentacles too.

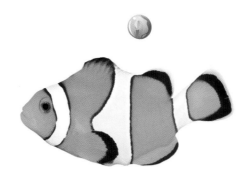

Life Cycle

Female clown fish lay
hundreds of eggs at a time.
Male clown fish keep the
eggs clean and safe.
The young fish hatch after
about one week.

19

Young clown fish float in the
ocean for many days.
Then they look for a sea
anemone to call "home."

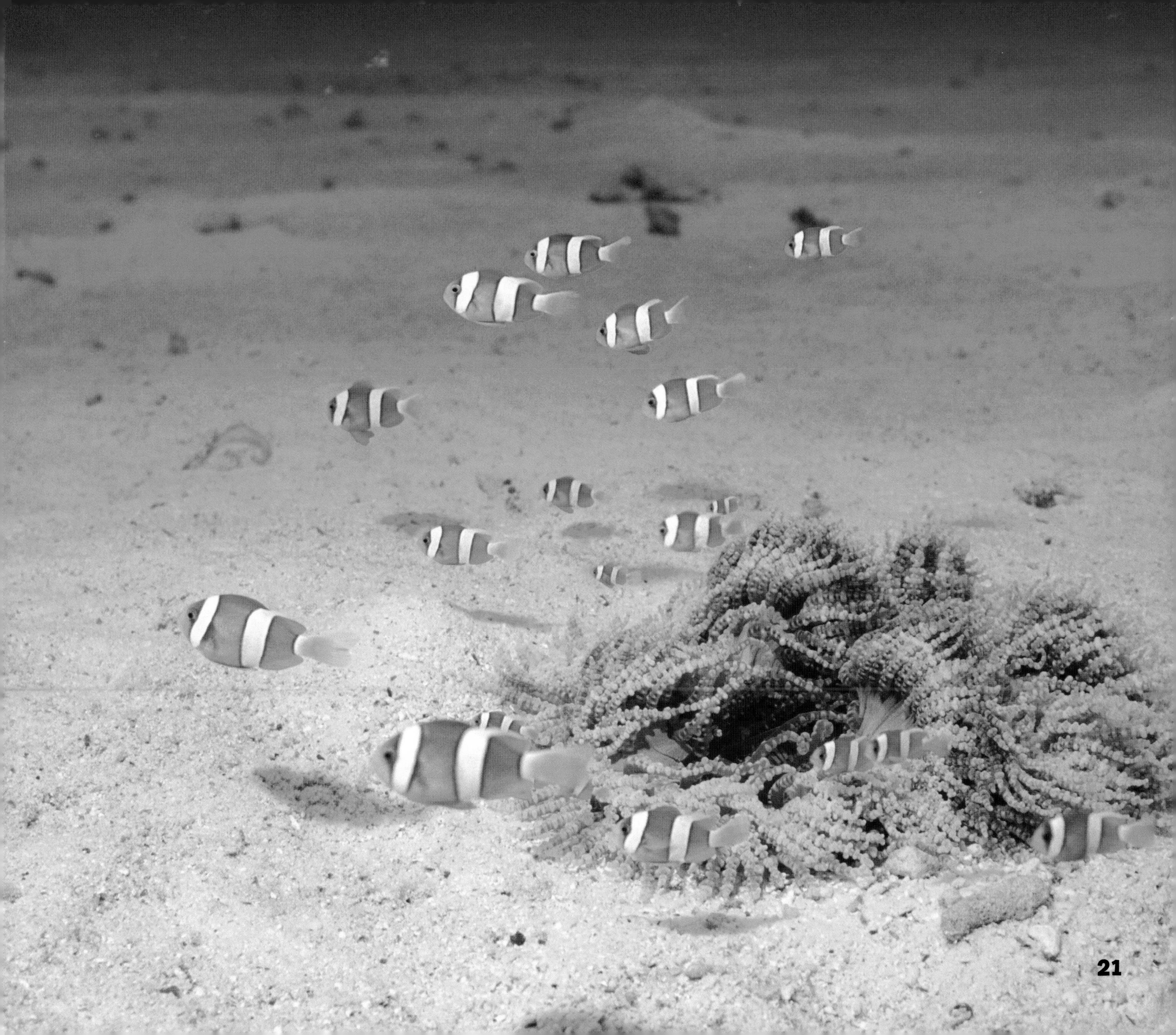

Glossary

coral reef—a type of land close to the surface of the ocean made up of the hardened bodies of corals; corals are small, colorful sea creatures

hatch—to break out of an egg

predator—an animal that hunts other animals for food

protect—to guard or keep something safe from harm

scale—one of the small, thin plates that cover the bodies of fish

sea anemone—a sea animal with a tube-shaped body and many tentacles

slime—a soft, slippery substance

stinger—a sharp, pointy part of an animal that can be used to sting

tentacle—a long, flexible body part used for moving, feeling, and grabbing

Read More

Gibbs, Maddie. *Clownfish.* Fun Fish. New York: PowerKids Press, 2014.

Martin, Isabel. *Fish: A Question and Answer Book.* Animal Kingdom Questions and Answers. North Mankato, Minn.: Capstone Press, 2015.

Owens, L. L. *The Life Cycle of a Clown Fish.* Mankato, Minn.: Child's World, 2012.

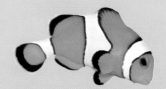

Internet Sites

FactHound offers a safe, fun way to find Internet sites related to this book. All of the sites on FactHound have been researched by our staff.

Here's all you do:

Visit *www.facthound.com*

Type in this code: 9781491460429

 Check out projects, games and lots more at **www.capstonekids.com**

Index

Word Count: 194

Grade: 1

Early-Intervention Level: 13